WHAT IS THE BOOK OF ISAIAH?

Kids' Guides to God's Word Series

What Is the Book of Genesis?
What Is the Book of Exodus?
What Is the Book of Leviticus?
What Is the Book of Numbers?
What Is the Book of Deuteronomy?
What Is the Book of Joshua?
What Is the Book of Judges?
What Is the Book of Ruth?
What Is the Book of 1 Samuel?
What Is the Book of 2 Samuel?
What Is the Book of 1 Kings?
What Is the Book of 2 Kings?
What Are the Books of 1–2 Chronicles?
What Are the Books of Ezra & Nehemiah?
What Is the Book of Esther?
What Is the Book of Job?
What Is the Book of Psalms?
What Is the Book of Proverbs?
What Is the Book of Ecclesiastes?
What Are the Books of Song of Songs &
Lamentations?
What Is the Book of Isaiah?
What Is the Book of Jeremiah?
What Is the Book of Ezekiel?
What Is the Book of Daniel?
What Are the Books of Hosea–Micah?
What Are the Books of Nahum–Malachi?

What Is the Gospel of Matthew?
What Is the Gospel of Mark?
What Is the Gospel of Luke?
What Is the Gospel of John?
What Is the Book of Acts?
What Is the Book of Romans?
What Is the Book of 1 Corinthians?
What Is the Book of 2 Corinthians?
What Is the Book of Galatians?
What Is the Book of Ephesians?
What Is the Book of Philippians?
What Are the Books of Colossians
& Philemon?
What Are the Books of 1–2 Thessalonians?
What Are the Books of 1–2 Timothy & Titus?
What Is the Book of Hebrews?
What Is the Book of James?
What Are the Books of 1–2 Peter & Jude?
What Are the Books of 1-3 John?
What Is the Book of Revelation?

What Is the Book of
ISAIAH?

Michael Whitworth

ISBN 978-1-944704-80-3

Published by Start2Finish
Bend, Oregon 97702
start2finish.org

Printed in the United States of America
30 29 28 27 26   1 2 3 4 5

CONTENTS

INTRODUCTION

Think about the teacher who changed your life. Not the easy one who let you coast. The one who was hard on you. The one who handed back your paper covered in red ink and said, "You can do better than this." The one who made you redo the assignment, not because she enjoyed watching you struggle, but because she knew what you were capable of and refused to let you settle for less.

Now think about what happened when things got really bad. When your parents were going through something. When you lost someone. When the bottom dropped out. That same tough teacher was the one who pulled you aside, looked you in the eye, and said, "I'm here. You're going to make it through this. I'm not going anywhere."

Same person. Same voice. Two very different messages, but the same heart behind both of them.

That's the book of Isaiah. It is the longest prophetic book in the Bible, and it sounds like two completely different books. The first half thunders with judgment. God brings charges against his people like a prosecutor in a courtroom.

He calls them rebels, hypocrites, a vineyard that produced rotten fruit. He warns that armies are coming, that cities will burn, that exile is certain. It's relentless. It's uncomfortable. It pulls no punches.

And then the tone shifts. "Comfort, comfort my people, says your God." Suddenly the same voice that was prosecuting is now consoling. The same God who announced judgment now promises restoration. Sins like scarlet will be made white as snow. The blind will see. The lame will leap. The dead will live. A servant will bear the sins of the world. Death itself will be swallowed up forever. And at the very end, God will create new heavens and a new earth where sorrow is a memory and joy never ends.

Same God. Same voice. Two very different messages, but the same heart behind both of them.

If you read only the first half of Isaiah, you'll think God is angry and nothing else. If you read only the second half, you'll think God is gentle and nothing else. You need both to understand who he really is: a God whose love is so fierce that he will not ignore what's destroying his people, and so deep that he will pay the ultimate price to bring them home.

WHY ISAIAH MATTERS

The prophet Isaiah lived and worked in Jerusalem during one of the most dangerous periods in Israel's history. He began his ministry around 740 BC, the year King Uzziah died, and continued for at least four decades through the reigns of Jotham, Ahaz, and Hezekiah. During that time, the world was being reshaped by the rise of the Assyrian Empire, the most brutal military machine the ancient world had ever seen. Nation after nation fell before Assyria's armies. The northern kingdom of Israel was destroyed in 722 BC, its people scattered and never heard from again. Judah, the southern kingdom where Isaiah lived, survived, but barely. By the time Sennacherib's army camped outside Jerusalem's walls in 701 BC, almost every other city in Judah had already been conquered.

Isaiah spoke into that crisis. But he also spoke beyond it. He saw further into the future than almost any other prophet in the Old Testament. He predicted the rise and fall of Babylon, named a Persian king called Cyrus more than a century before Cyrus was born, and described the suffering and death of God's servant in terms so precise that the earliest Christians read the passage and recognized the cross.

The New Testament quotes Isaiah more than any other Old Testament book except the Psalms. When John the Baptist announced Jesus, he used Isaiah's words. When Jesus launched his ministry in Nazareth, he read from Isaiah's scroll. When Philip met the Ethiopian official on a desert road, the man was reading Isaiah. When Paul explained the gospel to the Romans, he reached for Isaiah. This book is woven so deeply into the fabric of the New Testament that you cannot fully understand Jesus without it.

WHERE WE ARE IN THE STORY

To understand why Isaiah's message was necessary, you need to know where the story stood. God had rescued his people from slavery in Egypt, brought them through the wilderness, and settled them in the land he promised to Abraham. He gave them his law at Sinai, his presence in the tabernacle, and eventually a king in David whose throne was supposed to last forever.

But by Isaiah's day, things had gone badly wrong. The people were still showing up at the temple, still going through the motions of worship, but their lives told a different story. The rich were exploiting the poor. Judges were taking bribes. Widows and orphans were ignored. The leaders trusted foreign alliances more than they trusted God. And underneath it all, the slow poison of idolatry was eating away at the nation's soul.

God sent Isaiah to confront all of it. Not because he had given up on his people, but because he hadn't.

WHAT YOU'RE ABOUT TO READ

Here's where we're headed in this book:

Chapters 1–5 open with God's case against his people, climaxing in the famous vineyard song where God asks, "What more could I have done for my vineyard?"

Chapters 6–12 tell the story of Isaiah's calling in the temple, the crisis with King Ahaz, and some of the most stunning messianic prophecies ever written: "For to us a child is born," and "A shoot will come up from the stump of Jesse."

Chapters 13–27 broaden the view to include God's messages to the nations of the ancient world, and build to a vision of a feast on God's mountain where death itself is swallowed up forever.

Chapters 28–35 return to the question that haunts the entire book: will God's people trust him or trust something else?

Chapters 36–39 tell the dramatic story of King Hezekiah, the Assyrian siege of Jerusalem, and the fateful decision that set the stage for everything that follows. These four chapters are the hinge of the entire book. Everything before them looks toward the Assyrian crisis. Everything after looks toward Babylon.

Chapters 40–48 open the second great movement of the book with the words "Comfort, comfort my people." Here God declares that he alone is God, that idols are nothing, and that he will use a pagan king named Cyrus to bring his people home.

Chapters 49–55 contain the climax of the entire book: the suffering servant of chapter 53, who is pierced for our transgressions and crushed for our iniquities, followed by the great invitation of chapter 55 to come and drink freely from the waters of grace.

Chapters 56–66 carry the vision all the way to its conclusion: new heavens and a new earth, a world where wolves lie down with lambs, where God wipes every tear from every face, and where his presence fills creation the way light fills a room.

BEFORE YOU START

A few things to keep in mind before you start.

Isaiah is long. Sixty-six chapters, more than any other prophet. Some sections move quickly through dramatic stories. Others slow down into dense poetry that takes patience to absorb. Both kinds matter.

Isaiah deals with hard things. War, exile, suffering, the failure of leaders, the silence of God. These are not easy topics, but they are honest ones. Isaiah never pretends that life with God is simple. He shows us a world where faithfulness is costly and where God's people often choose the wrong path. But he also shows us a God who doesn't walk away.

Isaiah points to Jesus on nearly every page. The Immanuel prophecy, the child called Wonderful Counselor, the shoot from Jesse's stump, the suffering servant, the anointed preacher of good news, the one who proclaims the year of the Lord's favor. Thread after thread leads to the same place: a stable in Bethlehem, a cross on a hill, and an empty tomb.

And Isaiah ends where the whole Bible ends: with a new creation. The garden that was lost in Genesis is restored in Isaiah 65. The curse that fell in Eden is lifted. The story that began with God walking with his people in the cool of the day ends with God dwelling among them forever.

That's where we're going. From courtroom to garden. From judgment to comfort. From a vineyard that produced rotten fruit to a new earth where every vine bursts with life.

The journey starts with a father who loves his children too much to let them destroy themselves.

Turn the page.

1

GOD'S CASE AGAINST HIS PEOPLE

Picture this. Your mom spends all Saturday making your favorite meal for your birthday. She bakes the cake from scratch. She decorates the kitchen. She sets the table with the nice plates your family only uses on special occasions. And when you walk in the door, she's standing there smiling, waiting for you to notice.

But you don't. You walk right past her, drop your backpack on the floor, pull out your phone, and disappear into your room without a word. No "thank you." No "this looks amazing." Not even eye contact. And it's not just once. Imagine doing that every day, for years. Imagine your mom pouring everything she has into taking care of you, and you treating her like she doesn't exist. Or worse, like you wish she didn't.

Now imagine how she would feel. Not just annoyed. Not just disappointed. Heartbroken. Furious. Both at the same time.

That's where the book of Isaiah begins. Except the parent isn't your mom. It's God. And the ungrateful child isn't one kid. It's an entire nation.

A FATHER TAKES THE STAND

Isaiah opens like a courtroom scene. God is bringing charges against his own people, and he calls heaven and earth as witnesses: "I reared children and brought them up, but they have rebelled against me." That word "rebelled" isn't a small word. It's the word you'd use for a child who doesn't just disobey but turns their back on everything their parent stands for. It's personal. It's painful.

And then God says something that should sting: "The ox knows its master, the donkey knows its owner's feeding trough, but Israel does not know, my people do not understand." Even farm animals recognize who feeds them. Even an ox knows enough to come when its owner calls. But God's own people? They can't be bothered. They've forgotten who he is. They've forgotten everything he's done.

If you've been reading through the Bible in order, you know exactly what God has done. He rescued these people from slavery in Egypt. He parted the Red Sea. He fed them in the wilderness. He gave them his law at Mount Sinai. He brought them into the Promised Land. He gave them kings, prophets, and blessings they didn't earn. He was a father to them in every way that mattered.

And they walked right past him.

WORSHIP GOD CAN'T STAND

But here's what makes Isaiah 1 more than just a list of accusations. God isn't just angry. He's grieving. "Why should you be beaten anymore?" he asks. "Why do you persist in rebellion?" The nation is described like a body covered in wounds from head to foot: bruises, welts, open sores that no one has bandaged or treated. The picture is of a people who keep getting hurt because they keep making the same terrible choices, and God is asking, "How much more of this can you take before you'll listen?"

By the time Isaiah began his ministry, Judah was in bad shape. The nation had recently been invaded and devastated. Cities were burned. The countryside was ruined. Only Jerusalem was left standing, and even it was barely holding on, like a small shack in the middle of an abandoned field.

You might expect that kind of suffering to drive people back to God. And in a way, it did. The people were still showing up at the temple. They were still offering sacrifices, burning incense, keeping the religious calendar. From the outside, everything looked fine. They were doing all the "God stuff."

But God saw through it. And what he said next is one of the most shocking speeches in the entire Bible.

"Stop bringing meaningless offerings! Your incense is detestable to me. New Moons, Sabbaths, and convocations. I cannot bear your worthless assemblies. Your hands are full of blood."

Read that again. God told his own people that their worship disgusted him. Not because they were doing it wrong in some technical sense, but because their lives completely contradicted everything they were doing at the altar. They showed up on the Sabbath with their hands raised in prayer, and those same hands had been used all week to cheat the poor, take bribes, and ignore the helpless. They brought animal blood to the altar while the blood of injustice was still on their hands.

God wasn't impressed. He was revolted.

The message was clear: worship without justice is not worship. You can sing all the right songs and say all the right prayers, but if you walk out the door and treat people like they don't matter, God isn't listening. Not because he can't hear you, but because he won't. "When you spread out your hands in prayer, I will hide my eyes from you."

Instead of more rituals, God told them what he actually wanted: "Learn to do right. Seek justice. Defend the oppressed. Take up the cause of the fatherless. Plead the case of the widow." In other words, stop performing religion and start living it.

SCARLET TO SNOW

And then, right when you'd expect the hammer to fall, something remarkable happens. God makes an offer.

"Come now, let us reason together. Though your sins are like scarlet, they shall be as white as snow; though they are red as crimson, they shall be like wool."

This is one of the most famous verses in the Old Testament, and it deserves to be. At the exact moment when God has every right to condemn his people and walk away, he turns to them and says, "We can fix this. I can make you clean. I can take the worst, most stubborn stains on your life and wash them completely away."

But the offer came with a condition and a warning: "If you are willing and obedient, you will eat the good things of the land. But if you refuse and rebel, you will be devoured by the sword."

Two paths. Two outcomes. The choice was theirs. And the mouth of the Lord had spoken.

A BEAUTIFUL FUTURE, AN UGLY PRESENT

Chapters 2–4 pull back the camera. If chapter 1 showed us the disease, chapters 2–4 show us how deep the infection runs, and they also give us a glimpse of the cure.

Isaiah begins with one of the most beautiful visions in the entire Bible. He describes a future day when God's temple mountain will be lifted above all other mountains, and people from every nation will stream toward it. "Come, let us go up to the mountain of the Lord," they'll say. God will teach the nations his ways. He will settle disputes between them. And then this: "They will beat their swords into plowshares and their spears into pruning hooks. Nation will not take up sword against nation, nor will they train for war anymore."

That's the destination. That's where things are headed. Weapons turned into farming tools. Wars ended forever. The whole world learning to live in peace under God's teaching.

But the present reality was the opposite of that vision. Instead of looking to God, Judah was looking everywhere else. They were piling up silver and gold. They were filling their land with idols, bowing down to things they had made with their own hands. They were trusting in military power, foreign alliances, fortune-tellers, anything and everything except the God who had actually promised to protect them.

So God announced a reckoning. Isaiah called it "the day of the Lord," and it would be a day when everything proud and self-important would be brought low. The tall cedars, the high mountains, the mighty ships, the fortified towers: all of it would be flattened. "The arrogance of man will be brought low, and human pride humbled," Isaiah wrote. "The Lord alone will be exalted in that day."

The judgment got specific. God pointed at the leaders of Judah, the men who were supposed to protect the poor, and said, "It is you who have ruined my vineyard; the plunder from the poor is in your houses. What do you mean by crushing my people and grinding the faces of the poor?" He pointed at the wealthy women of Jerusalem, who paraded through the streets dripping with jewelry and expensive perfume while widows and orphans starved. Their luxury came at someone else's expense, and God saw every bit of it.

But even in the middle of all that judgment, Isaiah dropped a promise that changes everything. Chapter 4 describes a day when God would wash away the filth of his people and cleanse the bloodstains from Jerusalem. A remnant would survive, not because they deserved it, but because God refused to give up on them. And over that purified community, God would create something like the cloud and fire from the exodus: a canopy of glory, a shelter from the storm, shade from the heat. God would be with his people again, not as a distant memory but as a living, protective presence.

The pattern is stunning. Judgment, then grace. Discipline, then restoration. Even when God announces the worst, he can't help pointing toward something better.

THE VINEYARD SONG

Then comes chapter 5, and it changes everything again.

Isaiah starts singing. Literally. He sings a love song about a friend who planted a vineyard. This friend did everything right. He chose the best hillside. He cleared away every stone. He planted the finest vines. He built a watchtower and carved out a winepress. He did every single thing a farmer could possibly do to ensure a great harvest.

Then he waited for grapes. And the vineyard produced rotten, stinking, wild fruit. Useless. After everything the farmer invested, the vineyard gave him nothing worth keeping.

"What more could have been done for my vineyard than I have already done for it?" the farmer asks. "When I looked for good grapes, why did it yield only bad?"

And then Isaiah reveals the twist. "The vineyard of the Lord Almighty is the nation of Israel. The garden of his delight is the people of Judah. He looked for justice, but saw bloodshed; for righteousness, but heard cries of distress."

The vineyard is Israel. The farmer is God. And God is asking a question that hangs over the entire book: *What more could I have done?*

He gave them everything. He rescued them, provided for them, protected them, taught them, loved them. And they produced injustice instead of justice, cruelty instead of compassion.

SIX WOES AND A COMING ARMY

What follows is a series of six "woes," each one targeting a specific sin that had taken root in Judah.

Woe to those who hoarded land and houses until no one else had anywhere to live.

Woe to those who got up early just to start drinking and partied until late at night, never once thinking about what God was doing in the world.

Woe to those who dragged their sin around like an animal pulling a cart, daring God to do something about it.

Woe to those who called evil good and good evil, who twisted everything until nobody could tell right from wrong anymore.

Woe to those who were wise in their own eyes, convinced they didn't need God or anyone else to tell them how to live.

And woe to those who were heroes at drinking wine and champions at mixing drinks, while using their positions to rob innocent people of justice.

Isaiah's sarcasm is sharp here. He calls these men "heroes" and "champions," but their only achievements are getting drunk and taking bribes. They are brave at the banquet table and cowards in the courtroom.

The chapter ends with a terrifying image. God whistles for a distant nation the way a farmer whistles for a dog, and that nation comes running. An army appears on the horizon: disciplined, tireless, unstoppable. Their arrows are sharp, their bows are strung, their horses' hooves are hard as flint. They roar like lions seizing prey. And when they're finished, all that's left is darkness.

The vineyard that rejected its owner is about to be trampled.

WHAT THIS MEANS FOR US

First, God cares about how we live, not just how we worship. It's possible to say all the right things on Sunday and live a completely different way on Monday. Isaiah's message is that God sees both days. He's not fooled by religious performance. What he wants is a life that matches the words.

Second, privilege increases responsibility. God didn't judge Judah more harshly than other nations because he loved them less. He judged them more harshly because he had given them more. They had his law, his presence, his promises, his protection. "What more could I have done?" God asked. The more you've been given, the more is expected of you.

Third, sin doesn't stay small. The six woes in chapter 5 show how sin progresses. It starts with greed. It moves to indulgence. Then comes mockery of God, then moral confusion, then arrogance, and finally the corruption of justice itself. One sin feeds the next. What begins as a thin cord becomes a cart rope that you can't break free from.

Fourth, God's grace is stubborn. Even in these darkest chapters, God keeps offering a way back. "Come, let us reason together." "I will wash away your filth." "I will create a canopy of glory." The door to repentance stays open even when it would make perfect sense for God to slam it shut. His patience is not weakness. It's love that refuses to quit.

TALKING POINTS

1. **God compared his people to children who rebelled against a loving parent.** Why do you think it's so easy to take the people who love us most for granted? How does that apply to our relationship with God?

2. **The people of Judah were very religious on the outside but unjust in their daily lives.** What are some ways people today might "go through the motions" of faith without it changing how they actually treat others?

3. **God's offer in Isaiah 1:18 is stunning: sins like scarlet made white as snow.** Why do you think God made this offer right in the middle of his accusations? What does that tell you about his character?

4. **The vineyard song in chapter 5 ends with God asking, "What more could I have done?"** How would you answer that question? What does it tell us about how far God is willing to go for his people?

5. **The six woes describe sins that build on each other: greed, indulgence, mockery, moral confusion, arrogance, and injustice.** Which of these do you see most in the world around you? Which one do you think is the most dangerous starting point, and why?

God has laid out his case. His people are guilty. The vineyard he planted with such care has produced nothing but rotten fruit. An army is on its way. Darkness is closing in.

But the trial isn't over. God hasn't finished speaking. And before the next chapter opens, a young man is about to walk into the temple and see something that will change his life forever.

Turn the page.

2

THE CALL AND THE PROMISE

On December 24, 1968, astronaut William Anders pointed a camera out the window of Apollo 8 and took one of the most famous photographs in human history. The crew had traveled farther from Earth than any human beings before them. They were orbiting the moon. And as they came around the far side, the Earth rose over the lunar horizon: a small, fragile, blue-and-white marble hanging in the blackness of space.

Anders later said, "We came all this way to explore the moon, and the most important thing is that we discovered the Earth." The astronauts had seen their home planet a thousand times in pictures. But seeing it with their own eyes, from that distance, changed something inside them. They suddenly understood how small they were and how vast everything else was. This experience was later given the name "the Overview Effect." It's the shift that happens when you see something so much bigger than yourself that you can never go back to the way you thought before.

Around 740 BC, a young man named Isaiah walked into the temple in Jerusalem and had his own version of the Overview Effect. He didn't travel to space. He didn't leave the building. But what he saw in that temple rearranged everything he thought he knew about God, about himself, and about his entire future.

THE YEAR EVERYTHING CHANGED

Isaiah tells us exactly when it happened: "In the year that King Uzziah died." That single sentence carried enormous weight for anyone living in Judah. Uzziah had been king for fifty-two years. He was one of the longest-reigning and most successful kings in Judah's history. Under his rule, the nation had prospered. The economy was strong. The military was powerful. For most of Isaiah's life, Uzziah had been the only king anyone knew.

And now he was dead. The throne was about to pass to weaker hands. Assyria, the most terrifying military power on the planet, was growing stronger by the year. The future looked uncertain and frightening.

It was in that moment of national anxiety that Isaiah walked into the temple and saw something that made every earthly king look like a footnote.

"I saw the Lord, seated on a throne, high and exalted, and the train of his robe filled the temple."

The earthly king was dead. But the real King was very much alive.

HOLY, HOLY, HOLY

Above God's throne hovered creatures called seraphim. Each one had six wings: two covering their faces, two covering their feet, and two for flying. Even these magnificent heavenly beings couldn't bear to look directly at God or stand fully exposed before him. They covered themselves in his presence.

And they were calling to one another: "Holy, holy, holy is the LORD Almighty; the whole earth is full of his glory."

In the Bible, when a word is repeated, it means the speaker is emphasizing it. When a word is repeated three times, it means the speaker has pushed the idea as far as language can go. The seraphim weren't just saying God is holy. They were saying he is completely, utterly, infinitely holy. There is no one and nothing like him. He is in a category all by himself.

The sound of their voices shook the doorposts of the temple. Smoke filled the room. Isaiah was standing in the presence of the living God, and the building itself was trembling.

UNDONE

Isaiah's response was immediate and devastating: "Woe to me! I am ruined! For I am a man of unclean lips, and I live among a people of unclean lips, and my eyes have seen the King, the LORD Almighty."

Notice what happened. Isaiah didn't walk out of the temple feeling inspired and confident. He walked in and fell apart. Standing before a perfectly holy God, he could suddenly see himself clearly, and what he saw terrified him. His lips were unclean. His people were unclean. And the gap between who God was and who Isaiah was felt like a canyon that could never be crossed.

This is what holiness does. It doesn't just make you feel small. It makes you feel exposed. Every hidden sin, every careless word, every selfish motive suddenly stands out like a stain on white fabric.

But God didn't leave Isaiah on the floor. One of the seraphim flew to him carrying a burning coal taken from the altar. The angel touched it to Isaiah's lips and said, "See, this has touched your lips; your guilt is taken away and your sin atoned for." The coal came from the altar, the place where sacrifices were made. Isaiah's cleansing came not from his own effort but from God's provision. God himself removed the guilt. God himself made Isaiah clean.

Then came the voice of God: "Whom shall I send? And who will go for us?"

And Isaiah, the man who had just been face-down in terror, answered: "Here am I. Send me."

A HEARTBREAKING ASSIGNMENT

But the mission God gave Isaiah was not what you'd expect. God didn't say, "Go tell my people the good news, and they'll listen." He said something far more troubling: "Go and tell this people: Be ever hearing, but never understanding; be ever seeing, but never perceiving. Make the heart of this people calloused; make their ears dull and close their eyes."

Isaiah was being told, before he even started, that most people would not listen. His preaching would not lead to a great revival. Instead, it would actually harden people who had already chosen to ignore God. The message would give them one more chance to respond, and when they refused, their hearts would grow even harder.

Isaiah asked the obvious question: "For how long, Lord?"

The answer was bleak: "Until the cities lie ruined and without inhabitant, until the houses are left deserted and the fields ruined and ravaged." In other words, until everything falls apart. Until judgment comes.

But then, almost as a whisper at the end, God added a promise. Even after the nation was cut down like a tree, a stump would remain. And in that stump was "the holy seed." Life would survive. Hope would endure. Even in the worst-case scenario, God was not finished.

THE KING WHO WOULDN'T TRUST

The next test came quickly. Isaiah 7 opens with a crisis. Two kings from the north, Rezin of Syria and Pekah of Israel, formed an alliance and marched toward Jerusalem. Their plan was to overthrow Judah's king and replace him with a puppet who would join their coalition against Assyria.

The king of Judah at this point was Ahaz, and he was terrified. The text says his heart and the hearts of his people "were shaken, as the trees of the forest are shaken by the wind."

God sent Isaiah to meet Ahaz with a message: Don't be afraid. These two kings are nothing but "smoldering stubs of firewood." Their plan will fail. But there was a condition attached. Isaiah told Ahaz, "If you do not stand firm in your faith, you will not stand at all."

God even offered Ahaz a sign, anything he wanted, to prove that God could be trusted. "Ask for it in the deepest depths or in the highest heights," God said. The offer was breathtaking. God was essentially saying, "Name it. I'll do it. Just trust me."

Ahaz refused. He dressed up his refusal in religious language: "I will not ask; I will not put the LORD to the test." It sounded pious. It was actually defiance. Ahaz had already decided to trust Assyria instead of God. He didn't want a sign because a sign might obligate him to believe.

Isaiah's response was sharp: "Is it not enough to try the patience of men? Will you try the patience of my God also?"

And then God gave a sign anyway, not for Ahaz, but for the future: "The virgin will conceive and give birth to a son, and will call him Immanuel." The name means "God with us." Ahaz didn't want God with him. He wanted Assyria with him. But God's plan didn't depend on Ahaz's cooperation. A child was coming, and his very name would be the answer to every fear.

LIGHT IN THE DARKNESS

Chapters 8–9 describe what happened next. Ahaz got his wish: Assyria came. But Assyria didn't just defeat Syria and Israel. It rolled over Judah too. The land was plunged into darkness, distress, and gloom. The northern territories of Zebulun and Naphtali, the regions most exposed to invasion, were humiliated and crushed.

And then, right in the middle of that darkness, Isaiah delivered one of the most stunning prophecies in the entire Bible. "The people walking in darkness have seen a great light; on those living in the land of deep darkness a light has dawned."

The light wasn't a policy change or a military victory. It was a person.

"For to us a child is born, to us a son is given, and the government will be on his shoulders. And he will be called Wonderful Counselor, Mighty God, Everlasting Father, Prince of Peace. Of the increase of his government and peace there will be no end. He will reign on David's throne and over his kingdom, establishing and upholding it with justice and righteousness from that time on and forever."

Read those titles again. Wonderful Counselor. Mighty God. Everlasting Father. Prince of Peace. No ordinary human being gets called "Mighty God" or "Everlasting Father." No ordinary king reigns "forever." Isaiah was describing someone who was both human (a child born) and divine (Mighty God). Someone who would sit on David's throne, but whose kingdom would never end.

This wasn't Hezekiah. This wasn't any king Judah had ever seen. This was a promise that reached centuries into the future, all the way to a stable in Bethlehem. And it's no accident that the region Isaiah named, the land of Zebulun and Naphtali, is the same region where Jesus began his public ministry. Matthew quoted this exact passage when Jesus started preaching in Galilee: "The people living in darkness have seen a great light" (Matthew 4:16).

The light that Isaiah saw was Jesus.

A SHOOT FROM A STUMP

But Isaiah wasn't finished. In chapter 11, he circled back to that stump from his temple vision and gave it a name. "A shoot will come up from the stump of Jesse; from his roots a Branch will bear fruit."

Jesse was David's father. By saying "the stump of Jesse," Isaiah was picturing the royal family of David as a tree that had been chopped down. The glory days were over. The dynasty would fall. But from that dead stump, a new shoot would grow. A new king would emerge, not from the power and prestige of Solomon's palace, but from humble origins, the way David himself had once come from a shepherd's field.

This king would be filled with God's Spirit: the Spirit of wisdom and understanding, the Spirit of counsel and power, the Spirit of knowledge and reverence for God. He wouldn't judge by appearances or make decisions based on rumors. He would defend the poor and the oppressed with perfect justice.

And then Isaiah painted a picture of what this king's world would look like: "The wolf will live with the lamb, the leopard will lie down with the goat, the calf and the lion and the yearling together; and a little child will lead them."

No more predators. No more prey. No more fear. A world where natural enemies live in peace, where the most vulnerable creature, a little child, is perfectly safe. Isaiah described a world where "the earth will be full of the knowledge of the Lord as the waters cover the sea."

This isn't just a nice poem about animals getting along. It's a vision of everything wrong with the world being made right. Sin undone. The curse reversed. Creation healed. Eden restored.

A SONG AT THE END

Chapter 12 closes this section with a song, and it's no coincidence that it echoes the song Moses sang after God brought Israel through the Red Sea. Isaiah saw a day when God's people would sing again, not because an army was defeated, but because God himself had come to dwell among them.

"Shout aloud and sing for joy, people of Zion, for great is the Holy One of Israel among you."

The Holy One who shook the temple in chapter 6 now lives among his people. The God whose holiness made Isaiah collapse in terror is the same God whose presence fills his people with joy. That's the journey of these seven chapters: from a terrifying encounter with God's holiness to a joyful celebration of God's presence. The same holiness that exposes sin also cleanses it. The same God who judges also saves.

WHAT THIS MEANS FOR US

First, an encounter with God changes you. Isaiah didn't walk out of the temple the same person. When you truly see who God is, it reshapes how you see yourself, your sin, and your purpose. You can't have a real encounter with God and stay comfortable.

Second, God cleanses before he commissions. Isaiah wasn't sent out while he was still guilty. God dealt with his sin first. The coal from the altar did what Isaiah couldn't do for himself. This points straight to the cross, where God dealt with our sin through the sacrifice of Jesus.

Third, faithfulness doesn't guarantee easy results. Isaiah was told from the start that most people wouldn't listen. God didn't promise him success. He promised him a mission. Sometimes obedience means speaking the truth even when nobody wants to hear it.

Fourth, when human leaders fail, God's plan doesn't. Ahaz refused to trust God. It didn't matter. God's promise of Immanuel moved forward anyway. No human failure can derail what God has decided to do.

Fifth, the shoot from the stump is the hope of the world. When everything looks dead, God brings life. When the family tree of David has been reduced to a stump, God grows a branch that will bear fruit forever. That branch is Jesus.

TALKING POINTS

1. **Isaiah's vision of God left him feeling "ruined."** Why do you think encountering God's holiness had that effect on him? What does that tell us about the difference between God and us?

2. **God cleansed Isaiah with a coal from the altar before sending him out.** Why is it important that God dealt with Isaiah's sin before giving him a job to do? How does that connect to what Jesus did for us?

3. **Ahaz refused to trust God even when God offered him any sign he wanted.** Why do you think it's sometimes easier to trust in things we can see (like a powerful army) than in a God we can't see? When have you been tempted to rely on something other than God?

4. **The titles in Isaiah 9:6 describe someone who is both human and divine.** Why do you think God chose to save the world through a child rather than through a conquering army? What does that tell you about how God works?

5. **Isaiah's vision of wolves and lambs living together describes a world without fear or violence.** What part of that vision do you look forward to most? What would it mean for the earth to be "full of the knowledge of the Lord"?

God called a prophet. He offered a king one last chance to trust him. He promised a child who would be called Mighty God and Prince of Peace. He described a kingdom where lions lie down with lambs and justice rolls over the earth like water.

But between the promise and the fulfillment, a long and painful road stretches out. Nations will rise and fall. Empires will crash like timber. And God will have something to say about every single one of them.

Turn the page.

3

GOD OVER ALL THE NATIONS

One of the oldest stories in Greek mythology is the tale of Icarus. His father, Daedalus, was a brilliant inventor imprisoned on the island of Crete by King Minos. To escape, Daedalus built two pairs of wings out of feathers and wax, one set for himself and one for his son. Before they took off, Daedalus gave Icarus a warning: don't fly too close to the sun. The heat will melt the wax and the wings will fall apart.

Icarus promised to be careful. But once he was in the air, the thrill of flying was too much. Higher and higher he climbed, drunk on the feeling of power, convinced that the sky had no limits. The sun grew hotter. The wax began to soften. And before Icarus could do anything about it, the feathers came loose, the wings collapsed, and the boy who tried to reach the heavens plunged into the sea and drowned.

The ancient Greeks told that story because they believed the universe had a built-in rule: those who reach too high get knocked down. They called it hubris, the kind of pride that makes a person think they can live without limits. And the punishment for hubris was always the same. The higher you climbed, the harder you fell.

Isaiah 13–27 tells a version of that story that is far bigger and far more real. Not about one boy with wax wings, but about entire empires that tried to set their thrones above the stars. Not about a mythological rule built into the universe, but about a living God who holds every nation accountable. And at the center of it all is a king who says, "I will ascend to heaven; I will make myself like the Most High," and is brought lower than the grave.

MESSAGES FOR THE NATIONS

Up to this point in the book, Isaiah has been focused mainly on Judah and Jerusalem. But now the camera pulls back. Way back. God doesn't just have something to say to his own people. He has something to say to the entire ancient world.

Chapters 13–23 contain a series of messages directed at the nations surrounding Israel. Babylon, Assyria, Philistia, Moab, Damascus, Egypt, Tyre, and others. One by one, God addresses the most powerful civilizations on earth, and the message for each of them is essentially the same: I see you. I know what you've done. And your days are numbered.

This might seem strange at first. Why would the God of Israel care about what's happening in Babylon or Egypt? Because Isaiah's God is not a local deity. He's not a tribal mascot who only matters inside Judah's borders. He is the Creator of the entire world, and every nation on earth is accountable to him, whether they know it or not. The Babylonians worshiped Marduk. The Egyptians worshiped Ra. The people of Tyre worshiped Baal. But none of those gods were real. The God of Israel was the only God there was, and he was running the show even when the nations didn't realize it.

These chapters also served a practical purpose for God's people. Judah was constantly tempted to form alliances with foreign powers for protection. When Assyria threatened, they looked to Egypt. When Egypt seemed unreliable, they looked to Babylon. Isaiah's message was blunt: Why would you trust nations that are themselves under God's judgment? Every kingdom you're leaning on is going to fall. The only safe place to stand is with the God who controls them all.

THE FALL OF BABYLON

The section opens with Babylon, and for good reason. Babylon was the ancient world's symbol of human pride. All the way back in Genesis 11, the people of Babel had tried to build a tower to heaven, declaring that they could reach God on their own terms. That spirit of arrogance defined Babylon for centuries.

Isaiah describes God summoning armies from distant nations, mustering them like a general preparing for battle. The day of the Lord is coming against Babylon, and when it arrives, "the stars of heaven and their constellations will not show their light." The sun will be darkened. The moon will not give its light. The whole created order shudders at what God is about to do.

But the most dramatic passage comes in chapter 14, where Isaiah sings a mocking song over the fallen king of Babylon. This king, who once made nations tremble, who conquered cities and filled the earth with fear, is now brought down to the grave. The dead rulers already there rise up to greet him with bitter sarcasm: "You have become as weak as we are! You have become like us!"

The king's pride is described in five staggering boasts: "I will ascend to heaven. I will raise my throne above the stars of God. I will sit enthroned on the mount of assembly. I will ascend above the tops of the clouds. I will make myself like the Most High."

Five times the king says "I will." Five times he reaches for the place that belongs only to God. And the result? "But you are brought down to the realm of the dead, to the depths of the pit." The one who tried to climb above the stars ends up lower than the grave. The one who wanted to be like God is reduced to a corpse thrown out like a rejected branch.

The lesson isn't subtle. Pride that sets itself against God always ends the same way. Always. It doesn't matter how powerful the empire, how strong the army, or how impressive the achievements. Icarus falls. Babylon falls. Every throne built on arrogance eventually collapses under its own weight.

NO NATION IS EXEMPT

The oracles continue through chapter 23, and the list of nations grows. Moab is brought low despite its pride. Damascus will become a heap of ruins. Egypt's wise counselors will be exposed as fools. Tyre, the great trading city on the Mediterranean coast whose merchants were like princes, will be forgotten for seventy years.

But something surprising happens in the middle of all this judgment. In chapter 19, after pronouncing devastation on Egypt, Isaiah suddenly looks into the future and sees something astonishing: "In that day there will be an altar to the LORD in the heart of Egypt, and a monument to the LORD at its border." Egypt, one of Israel's oldest enemies, will one day worship the true God. And it gets even more shocking: "The LORD will make himself known to the Egyptians, and in that day they will acknowledge the LORD."

Then comes one of the most remarkable verses in the entire Old Testament: "In that day Israel will be the third, along with Egypt and Assyria, a blessing on the earth. The LORD Almighty will bless them, saying, 'Blessed be Egypt my people, Assyria my handiwork, and Israel my inheritance'" (Isaiah 19:24-25).

Did you catch that? "Egypt my people." "Assyria my handiwork." God is claiming Israel's two greatest historical enemies as his own. The nation that enslaved Israel and the empire that terrorized it will one day stand alongside Israel as equal recipients of God's blessing. The God who judges the nations is also the God who loves them. His goal was never just to punish. It was always to bring the whole world home.

WHEN GOD SHAKES THE EARTH

Chapters 24–27 shift from specific nations to the entire planet. Scholars sometimes call this section "the Isaiah Apocalypse" because it reads less like a political commentary and more like a vision of the end of the world.

Chapter 24 opens with a scene of total devastation: "See, the LORD is going to lay waste the earth and devastate it; he will ruin its face and scatter its inhabitants." No one is exempt. Priest and people, master and servant, buyer and seller: everyone faces the same judgment. The earth "dries up and withers," the heavens "languish," and the cities fall silent. The music stops. The celebrations end. The gates are battered to pieces.

Why? Because the inhabitants of the earth have "disobeyed the laws, violated the statutes, and broken the everlasting covenant." This isn't just about Israel's law anymore. Isaiah is talking about something built into the fabric of creation itself: a moral order that every human being knows, deep down, and that every civilization has violated. The earth is under judgment not because God is angry without reason, but because humanity has systematically broken the relationship it was made for.

But even in the middle of this cosmic shaking, voices rise up. From the ends of the earth, people begin to sing: "Glory to the Righteous One!" Even in judgment, God's people find something to celebrate. The destruction of evil is good news for those who have been crushed by it.

THE FEAST ON THE MOUNTAIN

And then comes one of the most beautiful passages in the entire Bible. "On this mountain the LORD Almighty will prepare a feast of rich food for all peoples, a banquet of aged wine, the best of meats and the finest of wines. On this mountain he will destroy the shroud that enfolds all peoples, the sheet that covers all nations; he will swallow up death forever. The Sovereign LORD will wipe away the tears from all faces."

Stop and picture that. After all the oracles of judgment, after the devastating portrait of a world laid waste, Isaiah sees a party. Not a private dinner for Israel's elite, but a feast "for all peoples." Every nation, every tribe, every tongue is invited to the table. And the host is God himself.

But this isn't just a nice meal. Something is happening at this banquet that changes everything. The "shroud" that covers all nations, the universal grief and sorrow that death brings to every family on earth, is being destroyed. Death itself, the final enemy, the one opponent that no army and no empire has ever defeated, is swallowed up forever.

And then, as if that weren't enough: "The Sovereign LORD will wipe away the tears from all faces." Not some tears. All tears. The tears of the widow. The tears of the orphan. The tears of the parent who buried a child. The tears of every person who ever cried out to God in the dark and wondered if anyone was listening. Every single one, wiped away by the hand of God himself.

If that language sounds familiar, it should. The apostle John quoted this passage almost word for word in Revelation 21:4: "He will wipe every tear from their eyes. There will be no more death or mourning or crying or pain, for the old order of things has passed away." What Isaiah saw from a distance, the New Testament places at the finish line of all history: the moment when God makes everything new.

YOUR DEAD WILL LIVE

One more surprise waits in chapter 26. In the middle of a song about trusting God through difficult times, Isaiah makes a statement that would have shocked his original audience: "But your dead will live, Lord; their bodies will rise. Let those who dwell in the dust wake up and shout for joy."

Resurrection. In the Old Testament, this idea is rare and mostly hidden in shadows. But here Isaiah says it plainly. The dead will not stay dead. Those who trusted God and died without seeing his promises fulfilled will be raised to share in the final victory. Death does not get the last word. The grave is not the end of the story.

This is the answer to the question every suffering believer has asked: What about the faithful ones who didn't make it? What about the people who trusted God their whole lives and died before things got better? Isaiah's answer is: they're not forgotten. They will rise. They will shout for joy. God's promises don't expire when the people who believed them do.

Chapter 27 closes the section with God defeating the great sea monster, a symbol in the ancient world for the forces of chaos and evil. God tends his vineyard with care. He gathers his scattered people one by one. And a great trumpet sounds, calling the exiles home to worship on the holy mountain in Jerusalem.

WHAT THIS MEANS FOR US

First, God is sovereign over every nation, not just the ones that acknowledge him. Babylon didn't worship God, but God held Babylon accountable. The same is true today. No government, no institution, no system operates outside the reach of God's authority.

Second, pride is the sin that brings down empires. The king of Babylon's five "I will" statements are the purest expression of human arrogance in the Bible. Every time we put ourselves in the place that belongs to God, we are building our own version of that tower, and it will always come down.

Third, God's plan includes all nations. The vision of Egypt, Assyria, and Israel worshiping together is one of the most radical statements in the Old Testament. God was never interested in saving just one ethnic group. His heart has always been for the whole world.

Fourth, death is not the final enemy it appears to be. The feast on the mountain and the promise of resurrection tell us that the worst thing is never the last thing. God will swallow up death. He will wipe away every tear. And those who trust him will rise.

TALKING POINTS

1. **The king of Babylon said "I will" five times, each time trying to put himself in God's place.** What are some ways people today try to play God in their own lives? Why is this so tempting?

2. **Isaiah says God will one day call Egypt "my people" and Assyria "my handiwork," alongside Israel.** What does this tell us about how big God's love is? How should this shape the way we think about people who are different from us?

3. **The feast on the mountain is described as a banquet "for all peoples."** Why do you think Isaiah used the image of a meal to describe God's ultimate plan for the world? What does sharing a meal together represent?

4. **Isaiah promises that God "will swallow up death forever" and "wipe away the tears from all faces."** Which part of that promise means the most to you right now, and why?

5. **The promise that "your dead will live" was a radical statement in Isaiah's time.** How does the resurrection of Jesus confirm and expand this promise? How does believing in resurrection change the way you live today?

The nations have heard their verdict. The earth has been shaken. But from the rubble, a feast is being prepared, a trumpet is sounding, and the dead are being called to rise.

Now Isaiah turns his attention back home. Judah is about to face a choice: trust in human power or trust in God. And the answer they give will determine everything.

Turn the page.

4

WHO ARE YOU GOING TO TRUST?

Have you ever been so scared about something that you tried to fix it yourself instead of asking for help? Maybe you were failing a class and instead of telling your parents, you tried to cover it up. Maybe you were being picked on at school and instead of talking to a teacher, you figured you'd just avoid the hallway where it happened. Maybe you heard your parents arguing late at night and instead of saying anything, you just put your headphones on and tried to pretend everything was fine.

It's a natural instinct. When you're afraid, you want to do something. You want to take control. Sitting still and trusting someone else to handle it feels impossible, especially when the problem is big and the solution seems slow.

That's exactly the situation Judah was in during Isaiah 28–35. The most powerful military machine in the ancient world, the Assyrian Empire, was bearing down on them. Cities were falling. Armies were on the march. The people of Judah were terrified, and they wanted to do something about it. So they made a plan. They sent ambassadors loaded with treasure south through the desert to Egypt, hoping to buy an alliance with the only nation powerful enough to stand against Assyria.

It was a reasonable plan. It was a practical plan. It was the kind of plan that smart people in a crisis come up with every day.

And God hated it.

SIX WARNINGS

Chapters 28–33 contain a series of six "woes," each one a sharp warning aimed at the leaders of God's people. The word "woe" in the Bible is serious. It's the kind of word you'd use at a funeral. When Isaiah said "woe," he wasn't scolding. He was mourning, because he could see where things were headed and he knew the people wouldn't listen.

The first woe targeted the leaders of the northern kingdom, Israel. Their capital, Samaria, sat at the head of a fertile valley, and its leaders spent their days drinking and partying while their nation crumbled. Isaiah compared them to a fading flower on the head of a drunk man at a banquet, beautiful for a moment but about to be knocked to the ground. Samaria fell to Assyria in 722 BC, and Isaiah used it as a warning to the southern kingdom: this is what happens when leaders refuse to listen to God. Pay attention, because you're next.

The remaining woes zeroed in on the leaders of Jerusalem and Judah. They were making the same mistakes. They were drunk, but not just on wine. They were intoxicated with their own cleverness, convinced they could outsmart both Assyria and God. They had a plan, and they didn't want to hear from any prophet who might tell them it was a bad one.

THE CORNERSTONE

In the middle of the first woe, Isaiah delivered one of the most important images in the entire book. The leaders of Jerusalem had made what they called an alliance. Isaiah called it "a covenant with death." They thought their deal with Egypt would protect them when Assyria swept through like a flood. They were wrong.

But God didn't just tear down their false security. He offered them a real one. "See, I lay a stone in Zion, a tested stone, a precious cornerstone for a sure foundation; the one who trusts will never be dismayed."

A cornerstone is the first stone laid in a building's foundation. Everything else is built on it. If the cornerstone is solid, the building stands. If it's crooked or weak, everything above it eventually cracks and falls. God was saying: I have placed something in Zion that you can build your life on. It's been tested. It's precious. It will hold.

The New Testament picks up this image and runs with it. The apostle Peter quotes this exact verse and applies it to Jesus (1 Peter 2:6). Jesus is the cornerstone. He is the foundation that will never crack, the one solid place to stand when everything else is shaking.

But notice the condition: "the one who trusts will never be dismayed." The cornerstone only helps if you actually build on it. If you ignore it and build your life on something else, on your own plans, your own alliances, your own cleverness, the flood will eventually sweep it all away.

THE RECIPE FOR SURVIVAL

The heart of this entire section comes in a single verse, Isaiah 30:15. It's one of the most important sentences Isaiah ever spoke. "In repentance and rest is your salvation, in quietness and trust is your strength."

That's it. That's the whole strategy. Turn back to God. Rest in his promises. Be quiet instead of frantic. Trust instead of scheming.

For a nation staring down the barrel of an Assyrian invasion, this must have sounded insane. The enemy was coming. Cities were burning. And God's prophet was telling them to be quiet and trust? Where were the battle plans? Where were the supply chains? Where was the cavalry?

Isaiah wasn't saying that preparation and action are always wrong. He was saying that when your first instinct is to run to Egypt instead of running to God, you've already lost. The leaders of Judah were doing everything except the one thing that would actually save them. They were sending envoys through the desert with donkeys loaded with silver. They were negotiating treaties. They were buying horses and chariots. They were working around the clock.

And God's response was devastating: "But you would have none of it."

They didn't want rest. They wanted results. They didn't want to trust. They wanted to control. And because they refused the quiet strength God offered, they would get the chaos they chose instead. "You said, 'No, we will flee on horses.' Therefore you will flee! You said, 'We will ride off on swift horses.' Therefore your pursuers will be swift!"

There's a bitter irony in that. The very horses they were buying from Egypt to save themselves would become the horses they fled on when everything fell apart. The thing they trusted instead of God would become the instrument of their humiliation.

GOING DOWN TO EGYPT

Chapters 30–31 make the Egypt problem explicit. "Woe to those who go down to Egypt for help," Isaiah declared, "who rely on horses, who trust in the multitude of their chariots and in the great strength of their horsemen, but do not look to the Holy One of Israel, or seek help from the LORD."

Isaiah wasn't anti-Egyptian in some nationalistic sense. The problem wasn't Egypt itself. The problem was what choosing Egypt revealed about their hearts. They trusted in what they could see, measure, and negotiate. They preferred a treaty they could hold in their hands over a promise they had to take on faith.

And then Isaiah said something that cut to the bone: "The Egyptians are men, not God; their horses are flesh, not spirit."

That's the bottom line. Every human power, no matter how impressive, is just flesh. Flesh gets tired. Flesh fails. Flesh dies. But the Spirit of God does not tire, does not fail, and does not die. Trusting in Egypt over God was like choosing a candle over the sun.

Meanwhile, God compared himself to a lion standing over its prey, totally unintimidated by the shepherds shouting at it. No amount of noise would scare him off. He would come down to fight on Mount Zion, and when he did, Assyria would fall "by a sword that is not of man." Not by Egypt's chariots. Not by Judah's cleverness. By God alone.

A KING WORTH FOLLOWING

After all the warnings and woes, Isaiah turned his eyes toward the future. In chapter 32, he described a king who would rule with justice. Under this king, each leader would be "like a shelter from the wind and a refuge from the storm, like streams of water in the desert and the shadow of a great rock in a thirsty land."

Think about what those images mean if you've been living in a world of corrupt leaders. The people of Judah knew what it was like to have rulers who took bribes, who crushed the poor, who cared more about their own comfort than their people's survival. And here was Isaiah saying: a day is coming when your leaders will actually protect you. They will be shade when you're burning and water when you're dying of thirst.

This king wouldn't judge by appearances or make decisions based on rumors. He would see things as they truly were. Under his reign, the fool would no longer be called noble, and the scoundrel would no longer be respected. Right would be called right, and wrong would be called wrong. And the result would be peace, quietness, and confidence forever.

That promise echoes Isaiah 30:15 perfectly. The peace that came from trusting God would become the permanent reality of life under God's king. The rest that Judah refused in Isaiah's day would one day be the defining experience of God's people.

THE DESERT IN BLOOM

The final chapter in this section, Isaiah 35, is one of the most beautiful passages in the entire Bible. After the darkness of judgment in chapter 34, chapter 35 explodes with light and life.

"The desert and the parched land will be glad; the wilderness will rejoice and blossom. Like the crocus, it will burst into bloom; it will rejoice greatly and shout for joy."

The landscape itself is singing. Places that were dry and barren are suddenly alive with flowers. And the reason? "They will see the glory of the LORD, the splendor of our God."

Isaiah told God's people to strengthen feeble hands and steady weak knees. He told them to say to those with fearful hearts, "Be strong, do not fear; your God will come." And when he comes, "the eyes of the blind will be opened and the ears of the deaf unstopped. Then will the lame leap like a deer, and the mute tongue shout for joy."

Every disability healed. Every limitation removed. When Jesus began his ministry and people asked if he was the one they'd been waiting for, he pointed to exactly these signs: "The blind receive sight, the lame walk, the deaf hear" (Matthew 11:5). Jesus was doing what Isaiah 35 promised. The desert was beginning to bloom.

And then comes the highway. "A highway will be there; it will be called the Way of Holiness." This road leads to Zion, to the city of God, and it is built for the redeemed. No lion will prowl along it. No danger will threaten those who walk it. "The ransomed of the LORD will return. They will enter Zion with singing; everlasting joy will crown their heads. Gladness and joy will overtake them, and sorrow and sighing will flee away."

That last image is extraordinary. Joy doesn't just arrive. It overtakes you. It catches up to you from behind, like something you've been chasing your whole life that suddenly grabs you by the shoulders. And sorrow? It flees. It runs away. It's gone forever.

WHAT THIS MEANS FOR US

First, the hardest thing about faith is often the waiting. God told Judah their strength was in quietness and trust. That's hard to hear when you're scared. But faith doesn't mean doing nothing. It means refusing to let fear push you into trusting the wrong things.

Second, there is only one foundation that holds. Alliances, strategies, money, popularity: all of it is flesh, and flesh fails. The cornerstone God laid in Zion is tested and sure, and anyone who builds on it will never be put to shame. That cornerstone is Christ.

Third, God's future includes total restoration. The blind see. The deaf hear. The lame leap. The desert blooms. This isn't wishful thinking. It's a promise backed by the character of God. And it began when Jesus walked the earth, healing exactly the things Isaiah described.

Fourth, the road home is real. The Way of Holiness isn't just a nice image. It's God's promise that he will make a safe path for his people, from wherever they are to where he is. No enemy can block it. No danger can stop it. And the destination is everlasting joy.

TALKING POINTS

1. **Isaiah said Judah's strength was "in quietness and trust," but the leaders wanted action and control.** When you're facing

something scary, what's your first instinct: to try to fix it yourself or to trust God? Why is trusting so much harder?

2. **The cornerstone in Zion represents something solid and tested to build your life on.** What are some "false foundations" people your age are tempted to build on? What does it look like to build on Christ instead?

3. **Isaiah told the people, "The Egyptians are men, not God; their horses are flesh, not spirit."** What are the "Egypts" in our world today, the powerful things people trust instead of God?

4. **Isaiah 35 describes a world where deserts bloom, the blind see, and sorrow flees away.** Which part of that vision speaks to you most? Why do you think God gave us such a detailed picture of the future?

5. **The "Way of Holiness" in Isaiah 35 is a highway built for the redeemed.** What do you think it means that even "fools" could not get lost on this road? What does that tell us about how God guides his people?

The warnings have been given. The choice has been laid out: trust in flesh or trust in God. And now the story is about to take a dramatic turn. An Assyrian army is camped outside Jerusalem's walls, and a general is shouting insults at the living God. Everything Isaiah has been saying is about to be put to the test.

Turn the page.

5

THE MOMENT OF TRUTH

On April 13, 1970, astronaut Jack Swigert radioed a message from the Apollo 13 spacecraft that no one at NASA wanted to hear: "Houston, we've had a problem."

An oxygen tank had exploded. The service module was venting gas into space. Power was failing. The crew was more than two hundred thousand miles from Earth in a crippled ship that was quickly becoming a frozen coffin. Every expert who looked at the numbers said the same thing: the odds of bringing the crew home alive were almost zero.

The astronauts couldn't fix the problem themselves. They didn't have the tools, the power, or the options. Everything they'd been trained to rely on was either broken or shutting down. Their only hope was to trust the engineers in Houston to find a way to guide them home using equipment that was never designed for what they were about to ask it to do.

For four days the world held its breath. And on April 17, against all odds, the capsule splashed down safely in the Pacific Ocean. The crew survived because, when every other option was gone, they trusted the people who could see the bigger picture.

Isaiah 36–39 is the story of a king who found himself in exactly that kind of situation. Every ally had failed. Every strategy had collapsed. The most powerful army on earth was camped outside his city walls, and a general was shouting through a megaphone that resistance was pointless. Hezekiah, king of Judah, had no army that could save him, no ally that could rescue him, and no plan that could work.

He had one option left: trust God.

THE ARMY AT THE GATES

Chapter 36 opens with a single devastating sentence: "In the fourteenth year of King Hezekiah's reign, Sennacherib king of Assyria attacked all the fortified cities of Judah and captured them."

All of them. Every fortified city in the country had fallen. Sennacherib's own records, discovered by archaeologists centuries later, boast of conquering forty-six towns and deporting more than two hundred thousand people. The Assyrian army had rolled through Judah like a flood, and now it was camped at Lachish, Judah's last major fortress before Jerusalem. Hezekiah was, as Sennacherib himself put it, trapped "like a bird in a cage."

This was the crisis Isaiah had been warning about for decades. Hezekiah had joined an anti-Assyrian rebellion, counting on Egypt for military backup. Egypt had sent troops, but they were defeated. The alliance that was supposed to save Judah had crumbled. Everything Isaiah said in chapters 28–35 about trusting flesh instead of God had come true with brutal precision.

And now Sennacherib sent his field commander to Jerusalem with a large army and a carefully crafted speech designed to break the city's will to resist.

THE SPEECH THAT SHOOK THE WALLS

The field commander stood at the aqueduct outside Jerusalem's walls and delivered one of the most psychologically devastating speeches in the Bible. It was aimed not just at the officials who came out to meet him, but at every ordinary person watching from the top of the wall.

His argument was simple and ruthless: you have nothing left to trust. He started with Egypt. "You are depending on Egypt, that splintered reed of a staff, which pierces the hand of anyone who leans on it!" In other words: your ally is worse than useless. Lean on Egypt and you'll end up bleeding.

Then he went after their faith. He claimed that Hezekiah had offended his own God by tearing down local shrines and altars. "How then can you repudiate him and say to me, 'We are depending on the LORD our God'?" It was a clever twist. Hezekiah had actually removed those shrines because they were sites of idol worship. His reform was an act of faithfulness, not rebellion. But the field commander twisted it to make it sound like Hezekiah had insulted God.

Then came the most audacious claim of all: "The LORD himself told me to march against this country and destroy it." He was lying. But it was the kind of lie that could get inside your head, especially if you were scared. Had God really abandoned them? Had all those years of Isaiah's preaching been for nothing? Were they truly alone?

When Hezekiah's officials asked the commander to speak in Aramaic instead of Hebrew so the common people on the wall wouldn't understand, he refused. He wanted everyone to hear. He turned and shouted directly to the crowd: "Do not let Hezekiah deceive you. He cannot deliver you! Make peace with me. Come out. I'll give you vineyards and grain, a new life in a new land. Has the god of any nation ever delivered his people from the king of Assyria?"

The people on the wall said nothing. Not a single word. Hezekiah had told them not to respond, and they obeyed. In a moment when panic would have been natural, their silence was an act of trust.

A KING ON HIS KNEES

When Hezekiah heard what the field commander had said, he tore his clothes, put on rough sackcloth, and went straight to the temple. He sent messengers to the prophet Isaiah with a raw, honest plea: "This is a day of distress, rebuke, and disgrace. Perhaps the Lord your God will hear the words of the field commander, who has ridiculed the living God."

Isaiah's response was immediate: "Do not be afraid. God will deal with Sennacherib."

But the pressure didn't let up. Sennacherib sent a letter directly to Hezekiah, repeating the same arguments: no god has saved any nation from me, and yours won't either. Hezekiah took the letter, went up to the temple, and spread it out before God. Literally. He unrolled the scroll and laid it on the ground in front of the Lord.

And then he prayed one of the most remarkable prayers in the Bible. "O LORD Almighty, God of Israel, enthroned between the cherubim, you alone are God over all the kingdoms of the earth. You have made heaven and earth." Hezekiah started not with his problem but with God's identity. He anchored himself in who God was before he said a word about what was happening.

Then he laid out the situation honestly. Sennacherib had destroyed nations and burned their gods in the fire. But those weren't real gods. They were just wood and stone, things people had made with their own hands. Of course they couldn't save anyone.

And then the prayer reached its climax: "Now, O LORD our God, deliver us from his hand, so that all kingdoms on earth may know that you alone, O LORD, are God."

Notice what Hezekiah didn't say. He didn't say, "Save us because we deserve it." He didn't say, "Save us because we've been good." He said, "Save us so the world will know who you are." This wasn't a prayer about Hezekiah's survival. It was a prayer about God's glory. And that made all the difference.

GOD'S ANSWER

God's response came through Isaiah, and it was devastating in its confidence. God addressed Sennacherib directly in a mocking poem: the "Virgin Daughter of Zion" despises you. She tosses her head as you retreat.

God reminded the Assyrian king that every military victory he had ever won was something God had allowed. "Long ago I ordained it. In days of old I planned it; now I have brought it to pass." Sennacherib thought he was the master of history. He was the tool. The ax doesn't brag to the person swinging it.

And because Sennacherib had raged against God himself, God would put a hook in his nose and a bit in his mouth and drag him back the way he came. The hunter would become the hunted.

Then God gave Hezekiah a sign. For two years the people would eat what grew on its own from the devastated land. But in the third year, they would plant and harvest and eat the fruit of their own vineyards again. Out of Jerusalem, a remnant would survive and grow. The land would live again.

"He will not enter this city," God declared. "I will defend this city and save it, for my sake and for the sake of David my servant."

That night, the angel of the Lord went out and struck down 185,000 soldiers in the Assyrian camp. When the survivors woke the next morning, the camp was full of dead men. Sennacherib broke camp and went home. He never returned to Jerusalem.

Some time later, while worshiping in the temple of his god Nisroch, Sennacherib was murdered by two of his own sons. The great king who mocked the living God was cut down in the house of a god who couldn't protect him. The irony could not be sharper.

A PERSONAL CRISIS

Chapter 38 steps back in time to an earlier moment in Hezekiah's life. He fell gravely ill, and Isaiah came to him with a blunt message: "Put your house in order, because you are going to die."

Hezekiah turned his face to the wall and wept. He prayed, not with the soaring faith of his prayer against Sennacherib, but with the raw, desperate cry of a man who didn't want to die: "Remember, O LORD, how I have walked before you faithfully and with wholehearted devotion."

It wasn't a great prayer. But it was an honest one. And God heard it.

Before Isaiah had even left the palace grounds, God told him to go back with a new message: "I have heard your prayer and seen your tears; I will add fifteen years to your life." God also promised to deliver Jerusalem from Assyria, a reminder that this event took place before the Sennacherib crisis. Hezekiah recovered. A simple poultice of figs was applied to his boil, and the king who was at the point of death got up and lived.

Later, Hezekiah wrote a poem about the experience. In it, he described the despair he felt, the bitterness toward God, the tears, and then the turnaround. Looking back, he realized that his suffering had been purposeful: "Surely it was for my benefit that I suffered such anguish." The experience had deepened his faith, taught him humility, and drawn him closer to God.

THE MISTAKE THAT CHANGED EVERYTHING

Chapter 39 describes the moment everything went wrong. Merodach-Baladan, the king of Babylon, sent envoys to Hezekiah with letters and a gift, supposedly to congratulate him on his recovery from illness. In reality, Babylon was looking for allies against Assyria, and Hezekiah was a promising candidate. It was a diplomatic overture disguised as a get-well card.

Hezekiah was flattered. He showed the Babylonian envoys everything: his silver, his gold, his spices, his fine oil, his armory, his storehouses. "There was nothing in his palace or in all his kingdom that Hezekiah did not show them."

Isaiah appeared and asked two sharp questions: "What did those men say, and where did they come from?" Then: "What did they see in your palace?"

Hezekiah's answer was honest and damning: "They saw everything. There is nothing among my treasures that I did not show them."

Isaiah's response was a prophecy that would change the direction of the entire book: "The time will surely come when everything in your palace, and all that your fathers have stored up until this day, will be carried off to Babylon. Nothing will be left. And some of your descendants will be taken away, and they will become servants in the palace of the king of Babylon."

Hezekiah's reaction is one of the most troubling moments in Scripture. He said, "The word of the LORD you have spoken is good," and then added privately, "There will be peace and security in my lifetime." He was relieved that the disaster wouldn't happen to him. The man who had prayed so magnificently for God's glory was now content to let his children pay for his mistake.

This chapter is the hinge of the entire book of Isaiah. Everything before it has been looking at Assyria as the main threat. Everything after it looks toward Babylon. The exile that Hezekiah's carelessness helped set in motion is the catastrophe that chapters 40–66 will address. The comfort that opens the second half of Isaiah is comfort for people who have lost everything to Babylon.

Hezekiah passed the test with Assyria. He failed the test with Babylon. And the consequences would last for generations.

WHAT THIS MEANS FOR US

First, trusting God doesn't mean the situation won't be terrifying. Hezekiah trusted God, and he still had an army outside his walls and a general screaming insults. Faith doesn't remove the problem. It changes who you lean on in the middle of it.

Second, the best prayers start with who God is, not with what we need. Hezekiah's prayer against Sennacherib began with worship, moved to honest description of the problem, and ended with a desire for God's glory. That's a pattern worth following.

Third, God's deliverance often comes at the last possible moment. Hezekiah had tried everything else first. Egypt had failed. Tribute had failed. Diplomacy had failed. Only when every human option was exhausted did God act. Sometimes the waiting is the lesson.

Fourth, success in one area doesn't protect you from failure in another. Hezekiah's faith was extraordinary when facing Sennacherib but reckless when hosting Babylon. One victory doesn't make you invincible. The moment you stop depending on God is the moment you're most vulnerable.

Fifth, our choices have consequences beyond our own lifetime. Hezekiah's moment of pride set in motion a chain of events that led to the exile. What we do today affects people who haven't been born yet. That's a sobering thought, but it's also a reason to live faithfully.

TALKING POINTS

1. **The field commander's speech mixed truth with lies to try to break the people's faith.** How do you recognize when someone is using half-truths to discourage you? What's the best way to respond?

2. **The people on the wall stayed silent when the field commander tried to frighten them.** Why do you think Hezekiah told them not to respond? Are there times when silence is the strongest thing you can say?

3. **Hezekiah spread Sennacherib's threatening letter before God in the temple.** What does that act tell you about how he viewed prayer? What would it look like for you to "spread out" your biggest fear before God?

4. **Hezekiah prayed beautifully when Jerusalem was threatened but responded selfishly when told about the coming exile.** What do you think changed? Why is it sometimes easier to trust God with big, dramatic problems than with everyday choices?

5. **Isaiah's prophecy about Babylon at the end of chapter 39 shifts the direction of the entire book.** How does knowing that consequences can outlast your lifetime change the way you think about the choices you make today?

The test has been given. Hezekiah passed one trial and failed another. Jerusalem was saved from Assyria, but a darker threat now looms on the horizon. Babylon is coming. The exile is certain. The temple will be destroyed, and the people of God will be dragged from their homes into a foreign land.

It will look like the end of everything.

But that's when a voice will cry out in the wilderness with the most beautiful words in the Old Testament: "Comfort, comfort my people."

Turn the page.

6

COMFORT FOR A BROKEN PEOPLE

Charles Dickens' *A Christmas Carol* is the story of a man named Ebenezer Scrooge who has been shown, over the course of one terrifying night, the full weight of his selfishness and the devastating future it will create. By the time the Ghost of Christmas Yet to Come is finished with him, Scrooge has seen his own lonely death, his empty house, and a world that is better off without him. He falls to his knees, begging for a second chance.

And then he wakes up. It's Christmas morning. The sun is shining. The church bells are ringing. He's alive. He's not too late. Everything he feared could still be undone. Scrooge throws open the window and shouts to a boy in the street, laughing and crying at the same time, because the relief of discovering that mercy is still possible is almost too much to bear.

If you've been reading through Isaiah from the beginning, you've spent a long time in the dark. Thirty-nine chapters of warnings, judgments, woes, fallen cities, and stubborn kings. You've watched God plead with his people to turn back, and you've watched them refuse. You've seen Assyria roll through

Judah like a flood and Hezekiah foolishly open his treasury to Babylon. The last words of chapter 39 are a prophecy of exile: everything will be carried off to Babylon. Nothing will be left.

And then comes chapter 40.

"Comfort, comfort my people, says your God. Speak tenderly to Jerusalem, and proclaim to her that her hard service has been completed, that her sin has been paid for."

If the first thirty-nine chapters are the long, dark night, chapter 40 is Christmas morning. The window flies open. The music changes. God is not done with his people. He never was.

A VOICE IN THE WILDERNESS

The chapter begins with voices calling out. One voice says, "In the wilderness prepare the way for the LORD; make straight in the desert a highway for our God. Every valley shall be raised up, every mountain and hill made low." Picture road crews leveling terrain for the arrival of a king. The obstacles are being cleared. God is coming, and nothing will stand in his way.

Centuries later, a man named John the Baptist stood in the Judean wilderness quoting these exact words, announcing that the road was being prepared for someone greater than any king. The highway Isaiah described was being built, and the one traveling on it was Jesus.

Another voice says, "All people are like grass, and all their faithfulness is like the flowers of the field. The grass withers and the flowers fall, because the breath of the LORD blows on them."

This isn't depressing news. It's reassuring. Every power that has ever oppressed God's people, every empire that looked invincible, every tyrant who seemed untouchable, is just grass. It will wither. It will fade. It will blow away. "But the word of our God endures forever." Empires die. God's promises don't.

THE GOD WHO HAS NO EQUAL

Beginning in 40:12, Isaiah launches into one of the most breathtaking descriptions of God in the entire Bible. He does it by asking questions that have only one possible answer.

"Who has measured the waters in the hollow of his hand, or with the breadth of his hand marked off the heavens? Who has held the dust of the earth in a basket, or weighed the mountains on the scales and the hills in a balance?"

The answer is obvious. Only God. Only someone infinitely greater than creation could hold the oceans like a cup of water, stretch out the sky like a piece of fabric, and weigh mountains like pebbles on a scale. The point isn't just that God is big. It's that he is in a category completely by himself. Nothing and no one compares.

Isaiah pressed the point further. The nations? "They are like a drop in a bucket." The islands of the world? God could pick them up "as though they were fine dust." The greatest empires in human history, the ones that made people tremble, are to God what a droplet of water is to the ocean.

And then came the question that exposed every false god: "With whom, then, will you compare God? To what image will you liken him?" The answer is: nothing. There is nothing in all of creation that comes close. Not the strongest army. Not the brightest star. Not the most impressive statue crafted by human hands. God is incomparable, and anyone who worships something else is bowing down to a shadow.

EAGLES' WINGS

Isaiah knew his audience. These were not people who needed a theology lecture. They were people who were exhausted, afraid, and wondering if God had forgotten them. So he addressed their doubt directly.

"Why do you complain, Jacob, and say, Israel, 'My way is hidden from the LORD; my cause is disregarded by my God'?" In other words: why do you think God can't see what you're going through? Why do you act like he's lost track of you?

"Do you not know? Have you not heard? The LORD is the everlasting God, the Creator of the ends of the earth. He will not grow tired or weary, and his understanding no one can fathom. He gives strength to the weary and increases the power of the weak."

And then the passage everyone knows:

"Even youths grow tired and weary, and young men stumble and fall; but those who hope in the LORD will renew their strength. They will soar on wings like eagles; they will run and not grow weary, they will walk and not be faint."

The strongest people on earth eventually run out of energy. The fastest athletes eventually collapse. But the people who put their hope in God receive a strength that doesn't come from within themselves. It comes from outside them, from the God who never tires and never fades. And the promise isn't just about dramatic moments of soaring. It's about the daily grind of walking, one step at a time, without giving up.

THE IDOL FACTORY

One of the most surprising features of Isaiah 40–48 is how

much space is devoted to making fun of idols. Isaiah didn't just argue that idolatry was wrong.

He made it look ridiculous.

In chapter 44, he described the process of making an idol in excruciating, sarcastic detail. A man goes into the forest and cuts down a tree. With part of the wood, he builds a fire, warms himself, and bakes bread. With another part, he cooks a meal and eats until he's full. And with the leftover piece, he carves a god, bows down in front of it, and prays, "Save me! You are my god!"

Isaiah's punchline is devastating: "Half of the wood he burns in the fire; over it he prepares his meal … From the rest he makes a god, his idol; he bows down to it and worships. He prays to it and says, 'Save me! You are my god!' They know nothing, they understand nothing; their eyes are plastered over so they cannot see, and their minds closed so they cannot understand."

Think about that for a moment. A man uses the same log to cook dinner and to make a god. The firewood and the god are the same piece of wood. If you wouldn't pray to your campfire, why would you pray to a statue carved from the same tree?

Isaiah returned to this theme again and again because the temptation to trust in visible, tangible things instead of the invisible God was the root problem behind every other failure in Israel's history. The idols of the ancient world weren't just religious objects. They represented a worldview: the belief that power belongs to things you can see, touch, and control. Isaiah demolished that worldview by showing how absurd it was.

THE PAGAN KING GOD CALLS "MY SHEPHERD"

Then came the shock of the entire section. In chapter 44, God declared, "I am the LORD, the Maker of all things, who stretches out the heavens, who spreads out the earth by myself." He then listed the things he was about to do: rebuild Jerusalem, restore the cities of Judah, dry up the rivers that stood in the way of his plans. And then he named his chosen instrument for accomplishing all of this.

"[I am the LORD] who says of Cyrus, 'He is my shepherd, and will accomplish all that I please; he will say of Jerusalem, "Let it be rebuilt," and of the temple, "Let its foundations be laid."'" Cyrus. A pagan king. A Persian emperor who did not worship the God of Israel. And God called him "my shepherd" and "my anointed."

This would have been deeply unsettling for Isaiah's audience. God was saying that he would use a foreign ruler who didn't even know him to accomplish his purposes for Israel. "I summon you by name and bestow on you a title of honor, though you do not acknowledge me," God told Cyrus through Isaiah.

This was not an endorsement of Cyrus' religion or his character. It was a demonstration of God's absolute sovereignty over history. God doesn't need his instruments to understand what he's doing with them. He doesn't need permission from kings to use them. He moves nations like chess pieces, and the pieces don't have to know they're being moved.

And the reason? "So that from the rising of the sun to the place of its setting, people may know there is none besides me. I am the LORD, and there is no other."

Historically, Cyrus did exactly what Isaiah predicted. In 539 BC, he conquered Babylon and issued a decree allowing the Jewish exiles to return home and rebuild their temple. A pagan emperor fulfilled the word of Israel's God, more than a century after the prophecy was given.

GODS WHO GET CARRIED

Isaiah drove the contrast home one final time in chapter 46. He described the gods of Babylon, Bel and Nebo, being loaded onto the backs of weary animals as Babylon fell. The gods that were supposed to protect the city had to be rescued from it. They couldn't save themselves, let alone anyone who prayed to them.

And then God said to his people: "Listen to me, you descendants of Jacob. I have upheld you since birth, and have carried you since you were born. Even to your old age and gray hairs I am he, I am he who will sustain you. I have made you and I will carry you; I will sustain you and I will rescue you."

The gods of Babylon get carried. The God of Israel carries. That's the difference. Every other god in the ancient world was a burden its worshipers had to haul around, maintain, repair, and protect. But the true God picks up his people and carries them. From birth to old age, from their strongest days to their weakest, he does not set them down.

WHAT THIS MEANS FOR US

First, God's comfort isn't soft. "Comfort, comfort my people" doesn't mean God is letting everyone off the hook. It means he has dealt with sin and is now announcing restoration. Comfort in the Bible is not the absence of difficulty. It's the presence of God in the middle of it.

Second, nothing in this world compares to God. Not technology, not popularity, not money, not the opinions of people you admire. Every substitute for God is an idol, and every idol is just firewood that hasn't been burned yet.

Third, God uses unexpected people to accomplish his plans. Cyrus didn't know God, but God knew Cyrus. This should humble us. God is not limited to working through people who understand what he's doing. He can use anyone and anything to keep his promises.

Fourth, the strength God offers is not natural. It doesn't come from willpower or positive thinking. It comes from hope placed in the right person. When you hope in the Lord, you receive something you couldn't generate on your own: the ability to keep going when every natural resource has been spent.

TALKING POINTS

1. **Isaiah 40 opens with "Comfort, comfort my people" after thirty-nine chapters of mostly judgment.** Why do you think God placed the message of comfort here? What does the order tell us about how God works?

2. **Isaiah says the nations are "like a drop in a bucket" compared to God.** How should this change the way we think about the things that seem powerful or intimidating in our lives?

3. **The idol-making passage in chapter 44 is intentionally funny.** Why do you think Isaiah used humor to attack idolatry? What are some modern "idols" that would look just

as ridiculous if we described them the way Isaiah described carved statues?

4. God called Cyrus "my shepherd" even though Cyrus didn't know him. What does this tell you about how much control God has over history? Is it comforting or unsettling to know that God works through people who don't even realize it?

5. Isaiah 40:31 promises that "those who hope in the LORD will renew their strength." What's the difference between hoping in God and just trying harder on your own? When have you experienced strength that didn't come from yourself?

God has spoken comfort to his broken people. He has proven that no idol and no empire can stand in his way. He has named a pagan king as his instrument and declared that there is no other God in all the earth.

But comfort is not the only thing God's people need. They also need rescue. And rescue requires a rescuer. In the chapters ahead, Isaiah will introduce a figure unlike anyone who has come before: a servant who will bring justice to the nations, not through power, but through suffering.

Turn the page.

7

THE SERVANT WHO CHANGES EVERYTHING

Charles Dickens' *A Tale of Two Cities* is set during the French Revolution, when the streets of Paris ran with blood and the guillotine never stopped falling. At the center of the story is a man named Sydney Carton. By every measure that matters to the world, Carton is a failure. He's a brilliant lawyer who wastes his talent. He drinks too much. He drifts through life convinced he is worth nothing to anyone. The people around him mostly agree.

But Carton loves a woman named Lucie, and Lucie is married to a man named Charles Darnay. When Darnay is arrested by the revolutionaries and sentenced to die, Carton does something no one saw coming. He sneaks into the prison, drugs Darnay, switches clothes with him, and takes his place in the cell. Darnay is carried out unconscious and escapes to safety with his family. Carton stays behind.

The next morning, the man everyone considered worthless walks to the guillotine in silence. He doesn't fight. He doesn't protest. He doesn't try to explain who he really is. He goes quietly to his death so that someone else can live. His final thought, as Dickens imagines it, is: "It is a far, far better thing that I do, than I have ever done; it is a far, far better rest that I go to than I have ever known."

An innocent man dies in the place of a guilty one. A nobody becomes the hero. A life everyone wrote off turns out to be the most valuable life in the entire story.

That's Isaiah 53. Seven hundred years before Jesus was born, Isaiah described a servant who would be despised and rejected, who would go silently to his death like a lamb led to slaughter, and whose suffering would purchase freedom for the very people who looked away from him. When you read it, you'll understand why the earliest Christians opened this scroll and said, "This is exactly what happened."

THE SERVANT STEPS FORWARD

We've already caught glimpses of a mysterious figure called "the servant of the Lord" earlier in Isaiah. In chapter 42, he was introduced as someone who would bring justice to the nations, not by shouting or forcing his way, but gently, without breaking a bruised reed or snuffing out a flickering candle.

Now, in chapter 49, the servant speaks for himself. "Before I was born the LORD called me; from my mother's womb he has spoken my name." This servant was chosen before he took his first breath. His mission was planned before history even knew his name. God shaped him "like a sharpened sword" and "a polished arrow," hidden away until the right moment.

But then comes a statement that would have stunned Isaiah's original audience. God tells the servant that restoring Israel isn't enough: "It is too small a thing for you to be my servant to restore the tribes of Jacob. I will also make you a light for the Gentiles, that my salvation may reach to the ends of the earth."

Too small. Saving an entire nation isn't big enough for what God has in mind. This servant's mission extends to every people group on the planet. Every continent. Every language. Every generation. God's rescue plan was never meant for one tribe. It was meant for everyone.

CAN A MOTHER FORGET HER CHILD?

In the middle of these chapters, the people of Zion voice the fear that has been haunting them since the exile was first predicted: "The LORD has forsaken me, the Lord has forgotten me."

God's answer is one of the most tender passages in Scripture. "Can a mother forget the baby at her breast and have no compassion on the child she has borne? Though she may forget, I will not forget you! See, I have engraved you on the palms of my hands; your walls are ever before me."

Think about that image. A mother might forget. It's nearly impossible, but it could happen. God says even if that unthinkable thing occurs, he will not forget. He has carved the name of his people into the palms of his hands. They are permanently written on his body.

For Christians reading this centuries later, the image takes on a deeper layer. The one who would save God's people would indeed carry marks in his palms, not engraved by a tool, but driven there by nails.

THE MAN NOBODY WANTED

In Isaiah 52:13, God speaks again: "See, my servant will act wisely; he will be raised and lifted up and highly exalted." That sounds like a victory announcement. You'd expect what comes next to describe a conquering king on a golden throne.

Instead, you get the most shocking reversal in the Bible.

"His appearance was so disfigured beyond that of any human being and his form marred beyond human likeness." The servant would be so badly beaten that people wouldn't even recognize him as human. Kings would shut their mouths in stunned silence. This wasn't what anyone expected a savior to look like.

Chapter 53 opens with a question: "Who has believed our message? And to whom has the arm of the LORD been revealed?" The answer, at first, was almost nobody. The servant didn't arrive with trumpets and armies. He grew up "like a tender shoot, and like a root out of dry ground." Nothing impressive. Nothing that caught the eye. "He had no beauty or majesty to attract us to him, nothing in his appearance that we should desire him."

And then the verdict of the crowd: "He was despised and rejected by mankind, a man of suffering, and familiar with pain. Like one from whom people hide their faces he was despised, and we held him in low esteem."

The servant would be the kind of person people cross the street to avoid. Not a celebrity. Not a conqueror. A sufferer. Familiar with pain the way a worker is familiar with their tools. And the world's response? They looked away.

PIERCED FOR OUR TRANSGRESSIONS

Then comes the passage that changes everything. The people who once despised the servant finally understand what actually happened, and their testimony is devastating in its honesty.

"Surely he took up our pain and bore our suffering, yet we considered him punished by God, stricken by him, and afflicted." They had assumed he was being punished for his own sins. They were wrong.

"But he was pierced for our transgressions, he was crushed for our iniquities; the punishment that brought us peace was upon him, and by his wounds we are healed."

Every word in that sentence matters. *Pierced* for *our* transgressions. *Crushed* for *our* iniquities. The punishment wasn't random and it wasn't unfair. It was deliberate, and it was substitutionary. The servant took what we deserved so that we could receive what he deserved. His punishment purchased our peace. His wounds accomplished our healing.

And then the verse that summarizes the entire human condition in a single sentence: "We all, like sheep, have gone astray, each of us has turned to our own way; and the LORD has laid on him the iniquity of us all."

"We all" and "us all." No exceptions. Every person who has ever lived has wandered from God. And the weight of every one of those wanderings was placed on a single pair of shoulders.

SILENT AS A LAMB

The servant's response to his suffering is as stunning as the suffering itself. "He was oppressed and afflicted, yet he did not open his mouth; he was led like a lamb to the slaughter, and as a sheep before its shearers is silent, so he did not open his mouth."

No protest. No defense. No cursing his accusers. The most unjust trial in history, and the defendant said nothing. In a book full of powerful speeches, this silence is the loudest moment of all.

He was condemned by a corrupt legal process. "By oppression and judgment he was taken away." He died and was buried: "He was assigned a grave with the wicked, and with the rich in his death." And the witnesses add one crucial detail: "He had done no violence, nor was any deceit in his mouth." He was completely innocent. Every bit of his suffering was undeserved.

If the story ended there, it would be the most tragic story ever told. An innocent man destroyed by the sins of others, buried and forgotten.

But the story doesn't end there.

IT WAS THE LORD'S WILL

Verse 10 contains perhaps the most difficult sentence in the chapter: "Yet it was the LORD's will to crush him and cause him to suffer."

This wasn't an accident. It wasn't a plan that went wrong. God himself willed the servant's suffering because through that suffering, something was being accomplished that could be accomplished no other way.

"After he has suffered, he will see the light of life and be satisfied." The servant who died will live again. He will see the results of his sacrifice and be satisfied that it was worth it. "By his knowledge my righteous servant will justify many, and he will bear their iniquities."

That word "justify" means more than forgiveness. It means being declared right with God. The servant's suffering doesn't just erase the record. It changes the relationship. The guilty become the righteous, not because of anything they've done, but because of what the servant did for them.

The chapter closes with God himself honoring the servant: "Therefore I will give him a portion among the great, and he will divide the spoils with the strong, because he poured out his life unto death, and was numbered with the transgressors. For he bore the sin of many, and made intercession for the transgressors."

The one who was treated like a criminal will be honored like a conqueror. The one who was buried with the wicked will stand among the great. And even now, even after his suffering is complete, he continues to intercede for the very people whose sins put him there.

When the Ethiopian official was reading this passage in Acts 8, he asked Philip a simple question: "Who is the prophet talking about, himself or someone else?" Philip's answer began with this chapter and told him "the good news about Jesus." The earliest Christians saw Isaiah 53 and recognized the cross.

COME, EVERYONE WHO IS THIRSTY

After the weight of chapter 53, chapter 55 opens like a door thrown wide. "Come, all you who are thirsty, come to the waters; and you who have no money, come, buy and eat! Come, buy wine and milk without money and without cost."

This is the feast that the servant's death made possible. Everything that was earned on the cross is now offered for free. Not earned. Not deserved. Given. The invitation is as wide as it gets: *everyone* who is thirsty. No prerequisites. No entrance exam. Just thirst and willingness.

God follows the invitation with a question that cuts to the heart: "Why spend money on what is not bread, and your labor on what does not satisfy?" Why keep chasing things that leave you empty? Why keep working for what can never fill you?

Then comes the call to action: "Seek the LORD while he may be found; call on him while he is near. Let the wicked forsake their ways and the unrighteous their thoughts. Let them turn to the LORD, and he will have mercy on them, and to our God, for he will freely pardon."

Freely. Not reluctantly. Not after you've earned it. Freely.

And if anyone wonders whether God's plans are big enough to handle the mess humanity has made, Isaiah closes with this: "For my thoughts are not your thoughts, neither are your ways my ways, declares the LORD. As the heavens are higher than the earth, so are my ways higher than your ways and my thoughts than your thoughts."

God's plan is bigger than anything we can imagine. And his word, like rain falling on the earth, will accomplish exactly what he sent it to do. It will not return empty. The rescue plan described in these chapters will succeed. The servant's suffering will not be wasted. The invitation to come will not be withdrawn.

The section ends with a vision of joy: "You will go out in joy and be led forth in peace; the mountains and hills will burst into song before you, and all the trees of the field will clap their hands."

Creation itself will celebrate the day God's people come home.

WHAT THIS MEANS FOR US

First, Isaiah 53 is the clearest explanation of the cross in the Old Testament. The servant was pierced for our transgressions, crushed for our iniquities, and his punishment brought us peace. This isn't vague symbolism. It's a detailed description, written centuries before Calvary, of exactly what Jesus did.

Second, grace is free, but it wasn't cheap. The invitation in chapter 55 to "come, buy without money" is only possible because someone paid the price. The feast is free to us because it cost the servant everything.

Third, God's rescue plan has always been for everyone. "A light for the Gentiles" and "salvation to the ends of the earth" are not afterthoughts. They were part of the plan from the beginning. No one is too far away, too different, or too broken to be included.

Fourth, silence can be the strongest statement. The servant's refusal to defend himself wasn't weakness. It was the deepest kind of strength: the willingness to absorb injustice without returning it, trusting that God would make it right in the end.

TALKING POINTS

1. **Isaiah 53:6 says "we all, like sheep, have gone astray."** Why do you think Isaiah uses the image of sheep wandering off? What does it feel like to realize that everyone, not just "bad" people, has turned away from God?

2. **The servant was "pierced for our transgressions" and "crushed for our iniquities."** What does it mean to you that someone innocent would choose to take the punishment meant for someone guilty? How does this connect to what Jesus did on the cross?

3. **The servant was completely silent during his trial.** Why do you think he didn't defend himself? What does his silence tell us about his trust in God?

4. **Isaiah 55 invites everyone who is thirsty to come and receive what they can't afford.** What are you "thirsty" for in your life right now? How does knowing that God offers what matters most for free change the way you think about what you're chasing?

5. **God says, "My thoughts are not your thoughts, neither are your ways my ways."** When have you experienced something that didn't make sense at the time but turned out to be part of a bigger plan? How does trusting God's bigger plan help when life feels confusing?

The servant has suffered. The servant has died. The servant has risen. The feast has been spread, and the invitation has gone out to the whole world.

But Isaiah isn't finished. There is still one more question to answer: what does the world look like when God finally makes everything new? The final chapters of Isaiah will take us all the way to the end, to a new heaven and a new earth where righteousness is at home and sorrow is a memory.

Turn the page.

8

EVERYTHING MADE NEW

Frances Hodgson Burnett's *The Secret Garden* tells the story of Mary Lennox, a sour, lonely girl sent to live in a sprawling English estate after her parents die. The house is full of locked doors and secrets, and the grounds contain a walled garden that has been sealed shut for ten years. No one is allowed inside. The garden, like the family that owns it, is considered dead.

But Mary finds the key. She crawls through the ivy-covered door and discovers that the garden isn't dead at all. Beneath the dead-looking branches, green shoots are pushing up through the soil. Bulbs are stirring underground. Life has been waiting. All it needed was someone to come in, pull away the weeds, and let the light back in.

Over the course of the story, as the garden comes back to life, so does everything around it. A bedridden boy gets out of his wheelchair. A grieving father comes home. A bitter girl learns to laugh. The garden's resurrection pulls everyone and everything around it into something new.

That's what the final eleven chapters of Isaiah are about. After everything that has come before, all the judgment and the suffering, the exile and the servant's sacrifice, God opens the door to a garden. Not a walled English estate but a new creation. A world where the ruins are rebuilt, the outcasts are welcomed home, and everything that was broken is made whole. Isaiah has been building toward this from the very first chapter. And now, at last, we get to see what God has been planning all along.

THE DOOR SWINGS OPEN

Chapter 56 begins with a surprise. After fifty-five chapters of being told who is in and who is out, God throws the door open wider than anyone expected.

Foreigners who had always been on the outside of Israel's story? Welcome. "Let no foreigner who is bound to the LORD say, 'The LORD will surely exclude me from his people.'" Eunuchs who were barred from the assembly by the law of Moses? Welcome. God promises them "a memorial and a name better than sons and daughters; I will give them an everlasting name that will never be cut off."

And then God makes a statement that sums up his entire mission: "My house will be called a house of prayer for all nations." Not for Israel only. For all nations. The God who chose one family out of all the peoples of the earth did so because he always intended to bring all the peoples of the earth home.

When Jesus walked into the temple and overturned the money changers' tables, he quoted this exact verse. The temple was supposed to be a place where the nations could meet God. Instead, it had become a marketplace. Jesus was angry because the door that God had opened was being slammed shut by the very people who should have been holding it open.

THE FAST GOD ACTUALLY WANTS

But having an open door doesn't mean anything goes. Chapters 58–59 make it clear that God still expects his people to live differently from the world around them.

The people had been fasting and praying, putting on impressive displays of religious devotion, and then complaining that God wasn't responding. "Why have we fasted, and you have not seen it? Why have we humbled ourselves, and you have not noticed?"

God's answer was blistering. Their fasting was a performance. While they went without food for a day, they were exploiting their workers, fighting with each other, and ignoring the poor. Their religion looked good on the outside but changed nothing on the inside.

So God described the kind of fast he actually wanted: "Is not this the kind of fasting I have chosen: to loose the chains of injustice and untie the cords of the yoke, to set the oppressed free and break every yoke? Is it not to share your food with the hungry and to provide the poor wanderer with shelter, when you see the naked, to clothe them, and not to turn away from your own flesh and blood?"

Real worship, in God's eyes, has always looked like justice. It looks like feeding the hungry, housing the homeless, and defending the powerless. And when God's people live this way, the promises start flowing: "Then your light will break forth like the dawn, and your healing will quickly appear."

Chapter 59 pushed deeper. The problem wasn't that God's arm was too short to save. The problem was that the people's sins had built a wall between them and God. "Your iniquities have separated you from your God; your sins have hidden his face from you, so that he will not hear." God was not distant because he was weak. He was hidden because they had pushed him away.

But even in the middle of that devastating diagnosis, God refused to leave his people in the dark. When he looked and saw that no one was stepping up to fix things, "his own arm achieved salvation for him, and his own righteousness sustained him." God himself would do what no human could.

THE ANOINTED ONE

Chapter 61 introduces someone who speaks in the first person with the most extraordinary credentials: "The Spirit of the Sovereign LORD is on me, because the LORD has anointed me to proclaim good news to the poor. He has sent me to bind up the brokenhearted, to proclaim freedom for the captives and release from darkness for the prisoners, to proclaim the year of the LORD's favor."

This figure combines the roles of prophet, priest, and king into a single person. He is anointed with God's Spirit. He brings good news. He sets captives free. He announces the year of the Lord's favor, an echo of the great Jubilee from Leviticus, when all debts were canceled and all slaves went free.

When Jesus stood up in the synagogue in Nazareth and read from the scroll of Isaiah, this was the passage he chose. He read it aloud, rolled up the scroll, sat down, and said seven words that electrified the room: "Today this scripture is fulfilled in your hearing" (Luke 4:21).

Jesus was claiming to be this person. The anointed one Isaiah described. The one who would bring good news to the poor, heal the brokenhearted, and announce that the great reset had finally arrived. The reaction in the synagogue was mixed. Some were amazed. Others were furious. But no one missed what he was saying.

ARISE, SHINE

Chapter 60 is a burst of light so brilliant it's almost hard to look at. "Arise, shine, for your light has come, and the glory of the LORD rises upon you. See, darkness covers the earth and thick darkness is over the peoples, but the LORD rises upon you and his glory appears over you. Nations will come to your light, and kings to the brightness of your dawn."

The world is dark. That hasn't changed. But into that darkness, a light appears over God's people, and the nations begin walking toward it. Ships bring God's scattered children home from distant lands. Foreigners rebuild the ruined walls. The wealth of nations pours into the city. And at the center of it all is not a political empire or a military conquest but the radiant presence of God himself.

"The sun will no more be your light by day, nor will the brightness of the moon shine on you, for the LORD will be your everlasting light, and your God will be your glory."

The book of Revelation borrowed this image for its description of the New Jerusalem: a city with no need for sun or moon, because the glory of God is its light. What Isaiah saw from a distance, Revelation places at the finish line of history.

REND THE HEAVENS AND COME DOWN

Chapters 63–64 contain one of the rawest prayers in the Bible.

The prophet looks at the state of God's people, at their long history of rebellion and failure, at the ruins of the temple and the scattering of the nation, and he cries out: "Oh, that you would rend the heavens and come down, that the mountains would tremble before you!"

It's the prayer of someone who has run out of solutions. The people can't fix themselves. Their hearts are too hard. Their habits are too deeply rooted. Their leaders keep failing. And so the prophet throws himself on God's mercy with nothing to offer except honesty: "We are the clay, you are the potter; we are all the work of your hand."

This prayer matters because it shows us what real faith looks like when everything has fallen apart. It doesn't pretend things are fine. It doesn't offer excuses. It doesn't bargain with God. It simply says: we can't do this. You'll have to do it for us. And then it waits.

NEW HEAVENS AND NEW EARTH

God's answer to that prayer is the most sweeping promise in the entire book. "See, I will create new heavens and a new earth. The former things will not be remembered, nor will they come to mind. But be glad and rejoice forever in what I will create, for I will create Jerusalem to be a delight and its people a joy."

This isn't a renovation. It's a new creation. God uses the same word here that he used in Genesis 1: "create." He is going to make something from scratch, something so new and so complete that the old world won't even come to mind anymore.

And what will this new world look like? Isaiah gives us specifics that are almost painfully beautiful: "Never again will there be in it an infant who lives but a few days, or an old man who does not live out his years." No more children dying young. No more lives cut short. "They will build houses and dwell in them; they will plant vineyards and eat their fruit." No more working your whole life for something someone else takes from you. "Before they call I will answer; while they are still speaking I will hear." No more waiting and wondering if God is listening. He will answer before you even finish the sentence.

And then the verse that brings the story full circle: "The wolf and the lamb will feed together, and the lion will eat straw like the ox, and dust will be the serpent's food. They will neither harm nor destroy on all my holy mountain."

The wolf and the lamb from chapter 11. The serpent from Genesis 3. The holy mountain from chapter 2. Every thread Isaiah has been weaving for so many chapters comes together here. The curse is lifted. The predators lie down with the prey. The serpent is reduced to eating dust. Eden is restored, but bigger and better and permanent.

A MOTHER'S COMFORT

The final chapter of Isaiah closes with one last image of God that is almost unbearably tender: "As a mother comforts her child, so will I comfort you; and you will be comforted over Jerusalem."

After sixty-six chapters of thunder and fire, of courtroom speeches and battlefield imagery, of empires rising and falling, God compares himself to a mother holding her child. Not a general. Not a judge. A mother. The same God who shook Mount Sinai and destroyed Sennacherib's army gathers his people into his arms and says: I've got you. It's going to be all right.

The book ends with a vision of all nations coming to worship God together, keeping an eternal Sabbath in the new creation. The Sabbath that opened the story of creation in Genesis now closes the story of redemption in Isaiah. The world that began with God resting after his work of making all things ends with God's people resting in his finished work of making all things new.

WHAT THIS MEANS FOR US

First, God's family has always been bigger than one nation. From the welcome of foreigners in chapter 56 to the gathering of all nations at the end of chapter 66, Isaiah's vision shatters every boundary we try to draw around who God loves. The door is open. The table is set. Everyone is invited.

Second, real religion changes how you treat people. The fasting passage in chapter 58 makes it impossible to separate worship from justice. If your faith doesn't affect how you treat the poor, the hungry, and the powerless, it isn't the faith God is looking for.

Third, God's ultimate plan is not to fix the old world but to create a new one. The new heavens and new earth are not a patch job. They are a fresh start. And the promise is not just that bad things will stop happening, but that good things will never stop.

Fourth, the comfort God offers is personal. He compares himself to a mother cradling her child. Whatever you're carrying right now, whatever weight sits on your shoulders, God's response is not a lecture. It's an embrace.

TALKING POINTS

1. **God welcomed foreigners and eunuchs into his community in chapter 56, even though some laws seemed to exclude them.** What does this tell us about how God's plans grow and expand over time? How should this shape how we treat people who feel like outsiders?

2. **The fasting passage in chapter 58 says the worship God wants involves feeding the hungry, sheltering the homeless, and setting the oppressed free.** What are some practical ways you could practice this kind of "worship" in your everyday life?

3. **The prayer in chapters 63–64 is raw and honest: "We are the clay, you are the potter."** Why do you think God values this kind of honesty more than polished, "perfect" prayers? What would it look like for you to pray with that kind of openness?

4. **Isaiah's description of the new heavens and new earth includes no more infant deaths, no more stolen labor, and instant answers to prayer.** Which of these promises means the most to you personally? Why?

5. **The book of Isaiah ends with God comparing himself to a mother comforting her child.** Why do you think God chose this image for the very end of the book? What does it tell you about who God is and how he feels about you?

The book of Isaiah began with a courtroom. A father brought charges against his rebellious children. A vineyard produced rotten fruit. An army marched toward a nation that had forgotten its God.

But the book doesn't end there. It ends with a garden. A new creation. A world where wolves sleep beside lambs and children play near the dens of cobras without fear. A world where God himself wipes away every tear, answers every prayer before it's finished, and holds his people the way a mother holds the child she thought she'd lost.

Between the courtroom and the garden stands a servant. Pierced for our transgressions. Crushed for our iniquities. Silent as a lamb. Alive again. And through his wounds, everything is healed.

That's the book of Isaiah. Not a horror story. Not a history lesson. A love story. The longest, most patient, most relentless love story ever told, written by a God who looked at a world full of people running in every wrong direction, and instead of walking away, said:

"Comfort, comfort my people."

The book is finished. But the story it tells is still being written. And you're part of it.